Table of Content

Introduction- The Understanding

The recent events that have occurred involving police officers across America has renewed negative feelings of previous police -citizen interactions. These negative interactions continue to remain a scar on many communities. The scars are visible, and from the citizen's perspective, this has resulted in nationwide police protest, riots, and overall dissatisfaction with police, as well as diminished trust in police. Often, these isolated events overshadow the positive work that many police officers contribute to various communities. In most cases, the negative police interaction receives attention from the public and media, casting a dark cloud. The aftermath of a negative police interaction diminishes the already frail relationship between police departments and the community and creates a negative working environment for police officers in these communities.

Police who are patrolling may experience a range of emotions such as fear, anxiety, anger, trauma, and periods of depression. These emotions are a natural part of policing but may not be properly internalized by some police officers. Compound these emotions with the pressure of patrolling in an area that may have had poor police and citizen interactions. This is a situation that is almost always designed to fail, and places police officers in environments to possibly receive enormous amounts of scrutiny. It is almost impossible to succeed since there are limited forms of healthy communication and a lack of trust by both stakeholders-- the police and the citizens. Citizens have expressed similar ranges of emotions such as fear of safety, anxiety, and trauma when they are confronted by the police. Since both parties are expressing similar feelings, it would seem practical to create a line of communication.

During these phases of dismay, it is imperative the police use empathy, understanding, and elements of professional reasoning. I mention that police need to display these actions since it's our job to serve and protect the public. It is easy to point fingers, pass blame, and look for others to correct the issues. Unfortunately, the profession of policing has some institutional practices that need to change, such as patrol methods practices, unfair community policing, and inadequate methods of communication with diverse communities. Often, the burdens of change within a community such as healing and patrol initiatives are bestowed on lower-tier police officers. These are the officers who, with all due respect have the least amount of power and influence on the police department. However, LTPOs do have the power to change interactions with citizens and develop a better level of communication within communities they serve. Research has shown that LTPOs are seldom consulted for departmental decision-making, yet they are the main agent of community change for the police department. This is a major failure since they are the ones with the capability to make police department decisions a success (or not).

Unintentionally, it is easy to forget the stellar job that most police officers perform daily. The public may take for granted the sacrifice police officers make to serve and protect communities. Most citizens are not aware of the physical, emotional, and psychological hazards that are associated with being a police officer. Yet, they expect perfection from police officers, even when they respond to unfavorable calls for service. After years of being a police officer, I realized that many police officers join the police department to help communities, but they can eventually become a victim of the profession themselves.

I felt compelled to write this book after consulting with police officers from different police departments and other experts in the policing profession. We all collectively agreed that a different form of literature needs to be presented to assist police officers. By no means is this a professional diagnosis of the policing profession or a remedy for all police-related issues. Hopefully, this book will increase individual police officer's morale and add working tools to increase job performance efficiency. This reading is designed to show support, share research-based knowledge, provide

insight on police practices, and help police officers better

serve their communities. Police are the only ones who

have firsthand accessibility to change the perception of

themselves.

Chapter 1 - Challenges of the Job

The process that an individual embarks upon to become a police officer and complete the police academy is an accomplishment. There are normally over six hundred hours of classroom, practical exercises, physical training, firearms qualifications, and scenario-based trainings dedicated to transforming a normal citizen to a police officer. The policing profession is unique because it employs individuals from diverse backgrounds, races, genders, ethnicities, educational backgrounds, and life experiences to support the common goal of protecting and serving communities across the nation. Even with advanced academic courses, research-based scenario training, and physical conditioning, police officers will continue to confront unanticipated challenges on the job.

There had been a rising debate among social scientists as to whether policing is one of the most difficult professions. Other than those who serve in the military during war times, policing is the only profession where personnel can daily confront dangerous situations. That alone makes policing one of the most difficult jobs to perform. Police officers are trained in the academy to handle hazardous situations, and they develop keen instincts from field experiences. Naturally, over time, many of these experiences will affect police officers individually in different manners. Surprisingly, research has found that one of the most annoying aspects of policing is police communication with management.

Communication Issues

Although images of unity are displayed by most police departments, there is often a constant disconnect between upper management and LTPOs. Studies show that many police departments' upper management and LTPOs continue to struggle to communicate effectively within the department. This is concerning since today's police officer is more verbally expressive than police of past eras. Often, police officers will display their discontent through the lack of job performance, poor decision-making, and attitudes towards the communities they serve. Professionally, LTPOs recognize the importance of the chain of command but a hierarchical style of management over time isolates lower-tier police. In general, LTPOs understand that they are not going to make executive decisions within the police department, but they would like some input on issues and matters that affect them.

The uneven exchange of demands by upper management and the need to belong from LTPOs erodes trust within the organization. This unspoken action is a contradiction in an organization built upon the foundation of internal trust. Essentially, trust cannot be established without a mutual level of understanding to develop further advancements in their stakeholder relationship. In most relationships, regardless of the dynamics, all stakeholders require specific needs to be satisfied to invest completely into the relationship.

Currently, most police departments send directives, procedures, and crime prevention initiatives through the chain of command for LTPOs to adhere. Sometimes, these demands will be received openly by police officers, and other times, police officers take an aloof approach. In many cases, upper management is often disconnected from the issues patrol officers encounter on the streets. Mid-level police management wants to appear capable of handling the issues that occur on their level and meeting the needs of upper management as well as LTPOs. LTPOs have issues that they would like to present to upper management to assist them in effectively performing their job. Often, the issues confronting a police officer may require a lengthy amount of time and often their needs are not met. The unresolved issues of not having their needs met along with the upper management continuing to require more from LTPOs generates frustration and disdain towards police management.

These internal issues are generated by the lack of communication between upper management and LTPOs, which creates personalized feelings within some police officers. These feelings are sometimes displayed in the police officers' attitude towards their job performance and attitudes towards the public. This can be a dangerous opportunity for the downward spiral of a good police officer. Police officers can make poor decisions during a period of frustration with upper management. It is incumbent upon police management to recognize the signs of major strife within the police department and develop a viable solution to remedy the areas of concern.

Police Management

In an ideal scenario, a Police Chief would have risen through the ranks of a police department. The chosen one would have spent valuable time in the trenches while developing a keen understanding of police management. For the LTPOs, this person would

be the perfect voice that represents the unheard voices.
This person would bridge the gap between upper
management and police officers since they can
comprehend the needs of both stakeholders. The police
department should operate at optimum altitude since a
leader is in place that police officers can trust.
Unfortunately, in many cases, this doesn't happen, and
this dream never comes to fruition. LTPOs should
understand that upper management has a different
obligation to the department and many LTPOs do not
take this into consideration. With fairness to upper
management, there are several aspects of the policing
that extend beyond the realm of crime fighting.

To demystify some of the intertwined issues, it
is important to analyze both stakeholders' perspectives.
As LTPOs, their reality centers around the streets they
patrol and the mindset they must maintain to function
safely during their shift. The upper management of a
police department is usually disconnected from the
issues that occur on the streets. They tend to focus their

attention on administrative strategies to assist the police department in operating effectively. Upper management must appease the city council, community leaders, neighborhood planning units, and other political affiliations associated with the police department. This is where the plot of LTPO and upper management differ. The running joke among LTPOs when upper management attempts to satisfy all community stakeholders but not the needs of the police department is the "Art of Poli tricks." These "Poli tricks" are one of the key components that impede understanding between LTPOs and upper management.

Many LTPOs would just like for the police management to be open and honest which would make sense since the basis of policing is trust. For example, a police officer working in an activity district on a night shift finds nothing political about his job. This officer finds difficulty in understanding "Poli tricks" when he or she is working in hazardous situations to serve and protect the community. There should be a more transparent form of communication internally that connects all levels of the police department. This is the problem with most police departments' management and the disconnect with LTPOs. The police officers are not given a stake within the department, and this leads to a disinterest in the police department. What must be realized is that everyone has an important job to perform on their specific level and that it is also important to constantly reconnect as one unit.

Points to Remember

1. The police department is one organization, with internal stakeholders who have differing responsibilities. LTPOs are focused on the streets while upper management focuses on administrative issues.

2. Communication is a key component in the policing profession, yet there is constant ambiguity amongst the communication between

the police department, police officers, and the

community.

3.   The hardest part of the job may not be

patrolling but navigating the culture of police

management-always remains flexible and fluid.

Chapter 2 - Toll of Job

A vast amount of research has been conducted regarding the psychological, emotional, and physical stressors of policing. Many researchers have agreed that policing is one of the most stressful occupations. As discussed in the previous chapter, stress can impact how police officers make decisions. All police officers will internalize stressors of policing in a different manner. What remains constant is that the profession will take a toll and alter aspects of a police officer's personality.

The metamorphosis from a regular citizen to a police officer is gradual but constantly developing. From the moment a police officer enters the police academy, stress is induced in all forms of training such as physical training, firearms, academics, and scenario-based training. The entire training academy is designed to induce a stressful environment and assess how the recruits perform under these conditions. Reality begins to settle in mentally that policing is distinctively different from any other occupation.

The psychological transformation of a police officer is developed in multiple stages within the training academy, the field training program, and during the rookie phase. When you think of a police department, its members come from diverse backgrounds, life experiences, and moral beliefs. Therefore, it is imperative from day one of police academy training to expunge all police recruits' attitudes and egos, and while also breaking down their individual personalities. This phase of transformation allows for constructive criticism to be openly received by police recruits and the identity of the police department to be integrated. Police recruits must believe the vision, mission, and values of the police department before they can enforce laws.

The next phase in the psychological transformation occurs in the field training program. This allows for the police recruits to display their training skills in a semi-controlled natural setting. They must

show self-assurance in their ability to perform daily

police tasks and follow hierarchal instruction from the

Field Training Officer (FTO). The ability to follow

instructions from leadership in a natural environment

outside of the training academy helps to reinforce the

psychological transformation of new officers so that they

begin to trust something beyond their own principles.

Psychological Toll

The next major psychological change occurs

when new police officers have graduated from the

training academy and are patrolling the streets. By this

time, most new police officers have completely changed

from a normal citizen to a fully vested police officer.

They really believe in the value of the mission statement

and want to serve the public. This is the moment that

they realize citizens look to them for answers and need

solutions to their problems. As a police officer, when

you arrive on your first call for service, a million

thoughts are racing through your mind, and you are attempting to maintain your confidence. What you do realize is the power that has been bestowed upon you as a police officer and that people depend on you to make the correct decision that directly impacts their life. These thoughts either command new police officers to respect their power or take advantage of it.

I remember my first call for service without supervision. We completed daily roll call and began to walk towards the patrol vehicles. I inspected my vehicle and radioed to dispatch that I was calling into service. Within a few seconds, the dispatcher called my unit and dispatched me to a double shooting with both suspects on the scene. I responded back and stood by my patrol vehicle with a blank stare on my face. The older officers looked at me, laughed, and said, "Welcome Rookie." I then entered my vehicle and began to search my field notes and Standard Operating Manual (SOP). I was searching to find answers on how to handle a single shooting, better yet, a double shooting. When I arrived on the scene, I saw both shooting victims/suspects on the ground with weapons. I was in total dismay and did not know what to do. I am not quite sure when the older officers arrived on the scene and took control, but I can tell you I was so happy! That was my baptism into the policing world and my ultimate psychological transformation.

Admittedly, at the time, I was not prepared psychologically or mentally to handle certain calls for service without assistance. My experience was gained eventually through the rapid pace of answering calls in an active police district and making numerous mistakes that challenged me personally. One of the major challenges in policing is managing and constantly experiencing the emotions of unknown calls. The mental preparation it takes to remain alert is difficult but necessary when responding to domestic violence, assault, burglary, traffic stops, and hazardous daily job duties. For example, if an officer is patrolling in a high crime area and repeatedly responding to crimes of a violent nature, these types of calls in such a short period of time can create burnout. It is psychologically taxing trying to match the demands of the visual scenes, internal emotions, and mental energy that the job demands. A healthy mental balance is needed to combat the physical and mental exhaustion that policing creates.

I was at a conference recently, and the topic of the session was the importance of the affirmation. I learned that individuals who receive affirmation tend to produce a better quality of work and that their attitudes influence other colleagues. The speaker discussed statistics which revealed that more workers would like to receive personal recognition than a monetary award. I then reflected on how the affirmation theory could intertwine with the concept of policing.

The mission of most police departments is to serve and protect the public with some variations of the motto. Traditionally, police will respond to a call for service and provide resolve to a situation. These scenarios could be routine calls or calls that could entail immense challenges. No matter the scenario, most police never receive a simple "thank you" for the services they provide. Of course, some will say that the salary an officer receives is "thank you" enough, but as humans, we all like to be acknowledged for our work.

Even if they do receive any acknowledgment for their work, there is another undeclared psychological factor that burdens police. The one fundamental piece of equipment which is a lifeline but also a detriment to police and their psychological state, is the police radio. This is a device that delivers nonstop negative information. Now, just imagine being a police officer who has to digest this information in their ear for 8, 10, or 12 hours on a regular basis. Additionally, think about the police officer who has responded to calls for the past 3 to 5 years in an active district. After years of visually witnessing and audibly hearing negative information, and responding to calls for service, there becomes a level of psychological numbness that develops.

Maintaining a healthy psychological balance may be difficult during periods of policing. Police have been given the task of being a modern-day superhero and saving the day for normal citizens. Many police officers are internally reaching out for help, but often, people miss the signs. The culture of the profession does not want to display a sign of weakness within the blue line. Many officers seek to remain intact within the culture by emotionally suppressing their feelings in order to maintain the core values of the police subculture. This behavior is not recommended by mental health professionals since this concept can lead to a downward spiral psychologically for some police officers.

With certainty, there is no profession other than active duty military that mirrors the hazards that police officers encounter. These are the only professions that require its personnel to go towards danger and remedy a scene safe. Encountering constant danger for a living, at some point changes your personality. The key to maintaining a moderate level of normalcy necessitates an outlet for job-related stressors. Professionally, police cannot continue to conceal their emotions, feelings, fears, and the burdens of the job. A recent study revealed that the negative consequence of suppressing your emotions is that they appear in other aspects of your life.

Emotional Toll

A natural interaction between police and citizens daily can create a range of emotional responses such as negative, positive, or neutral stressors. When these emotions are experienced, they may often be internalized, which can generate a need to suppress, act upon, or develop mechanisms to control surging feelings. The ability to control and suppress your emotions is imperative during certain situations. The suppression of emotions is warranted to make an ethical decision in responsively charged situations. Therefore, police officers unintentionally practice the art of separating themselves from their natural emotions such as sorrow, fear, anxiety, and nervousness.

Professionally, it is good to maintain a fortitude presence in public, but personally, this posture can develop negative traits. Internalizing emotions is a natural part of policing, but the failure to properly release these emotions affect you personally. Some police officers isolate themselves and never discuss their emotions. Thus, police are encumbered with months, or even years of unresolved emotions which, if not properly released, may result in negative actions.

Since police officers rarely discuss the array of emotions they internalize, subconsciously they may develop unsafe coping mechanisms and self-diagnose. Historically, past research revealed that police cope by drinking, respond with quick tempers, stimuli-based activities, or exhibit other negative behaviors. While it appears simple to recognize and solve from a research-based perspective, emotional burnout is difficult to initially diagnose. This challenge arises because most police do not realize that they are emotionally exhausted until later stages of exhaustion. For example, there are external factors that complicate the analysis of emotional burnout.

When referencing emotional police burnout, it is imperative to understand the demographic area of patrol. Various demographics present police officer's challenges that are specific to the area of patrol. Police officers patrolling in a high crime area may experience crimes of a violent nature and a higher volume of calls during peak months. Often burnout can be confused with always having a constant heavy workload. Police officers patrolling in a low crime area may experience calls of a lesser violent nature, but implement a political style of policing which is stressful for them.

Another commonly recognized emotional burnout factor among police officers has been associated with the lack of resources, manpower, and equipment which often hinder police performance. As referenced earlier, these job-related concerns are factors in the uneven exchange of communication with the police department. Police are tasked to complete their job with a level of accurateness, but this is difficult without the proper resources. Now, I am sure other professions may operate with a lack of resources and these problems are common in many organizations. Then, I pose the question, are other occupations required to serve, protect, and maintain public order?

These factors are some stressors that confront LTPOs on a constant basis that is beyond their control. Police management's explanation for the lack of any resource will always be a result of budget reduction or reallocation of public safety funds. Professionally, I have no legitimate response for why government officials would allow for shortcoming in funds for public safety. Especially, when an emergency arises, police are expected to rise to the challenge. Therefore, it is important to realize the accountability of LTPO to the community and what they are expected to perform.

Decisions will be made by non-law enforcement officials that have a direct impact on the police department's operations and affect LTPOs job performance. It will be important not to personalize the decisions, and simply perform your job to the best of your ability. Often, when public officials make decisions that are not in favor of the police department, police tend to say the city/local government entity doesn't like police officers. Then, LTPOs take a disposition of rebellion against upper police management, sometimes unleashing frustration and unwarranted emotions on anyone within the path. These emotions are natural, being that it is your physical labor that supports community safety. In most relationships, you would like for all stakeholders to equally invest in the vision.

There may be a minimum investment by the police department but expectations of maximum return from LTPOs. This is a difficult circumstance for police officers, and several options are available. Some people will say you took an oath and the public depends on you.

Police officers may take a similar approach as government and invest minimum; the results will then also be minimum. Many will straddle the fence, with emotions varying daily. There is no correct manner to approach this scenario; the decision will be within your moral compass. The governing agency in most cases attempts to make decisions that are in the overall best interest of the governing entity. Most governing agency officials are oblivious to your daily rigors, and inflexible principles are focused on reducing the budget. The police department is just one jambalaya ingredient mixed with other working parts.

Physical Toll

The dark humor within the police culture says, "police will die within the first year of full retirement." Research reveals that the policing occupation has one of the shortest life spans for its personnel. Among themselves, police may laugh about not collecting their pension they sacrificed to earn, but it is a sad reality. The profession will take a physical toll on the body, spirit, and mind. The residual effect of the physical toll isn't determined until later years of your life.

Initially, all police officers are in great shape once they graduate the police academy. Most police departments across the nation stress the importance of physical conditioning and mandate a substantial portion of academy training to physical fitness. It is normally after police officers are assigned to police districts that physical fitness declines. Often, the decline is a result of changes in patrol shifts, off days, courts schedules, extra security jobs, and personal lives.

The abnormal patrol shifts are reported to defy the natural bio-rhythms of sleeping patterns. Many police officers work extra jobs either before or after their required patrol hours. These long days can be overall physically exhausting since policing requires mental alertness. With the constant evolving schedule, many police officers eat fast foods or food accessible to their schedule. Due to the lack of traditional sleep pattern and challenging nutrition eating habits, this creates the initial stages of physical fitness decline. The abnormal work hours and other job-related duties make it challenging to incorporate a regular workout schedule. An individual police officer must have a high level of dedication to maintain their fitness during these abnormal hours.

Research has shown that over extended periods of time many police officers become ill, suffering from cardiac and digestive health issues. These health issues have been associated the lack of proper nutrition, lack of adequate rest, and lack of physical exercise. Research has shown that these diseases are prevalent in police officers, due to the stressors of the job. Therefore, it is imperative to create and maintain a healthy balance early during a police officer's career and continue a healthy lifestyle.

The Unaware Change

Since policing invasively becomes part of a police officer's personal life, and they will always be known as a police officer even if they change professions. There are external factors police officers unconsciously encounter that alter their personality and cause them to isolate themselves due to the profession such as lack of trust in others, outsiders' lack of understanding, and obligation to live by a higher standard. Policing is one of the few professions where police are always considered on duty twenty-four-seven. Thus, many police internalize this philosophy and are always in a policing mode even on their off days. For example, think for a minute, have you ever seen a police officer that always has a badge and gun even off duty. I understand carrying off-duty to protect yourself, but professionally, police need to exhale.

To begin the professional exhaling process, police need to attempt to befriend people other than law enforcement personnel. Yes, it may sound weird, but police need to expand beyond their normal social network and meet other professionals with similar ethical standards to socialize. There are other trustworthy professionals in different social networks, and they may offer diversified friendships. This action of expanding your social network may slowly alter a police officer's perception of citizens. It should allow police to interact with others without automatically analyzing their disposition.

For example, a few years back, I was on a date in a nice restaurant, and of course, I positioned myself where I could see the door. My date was very engaging and had great conversation. After about thirty minutes of conversation, she stated, "do you realize that you have analyzed everyone that has entered into this restaurant." Always attempting to remain alert and ready to respond is a difficult mindset to discard, but it is good to relax mentally and attempt to be a normal citizen.

The inability to discard the police officer mindset is a difficult task to master but is very necessary for mental health purposes. By no means am I saying forget your tactical training, and you should always protect your family. But sometimes I think it is ok to put yourself first and think about your well-being. Most police need to find a healthy balance where they can completely allow themselves to relax. Policing can be such an intrusive profession that often police mentally approach their professional and personal life with the same outlook.

Finding a personal comfort zone for police may result in a trial and error period. The trial and error period may be initially uncomfortable but is needed to shape new dimensions in your life. Many studies references on discovering new things that are uncharacteristic of your personality. This activity will expand your horizons and liberate you to create new ideas. After you identify your source of comfort, then you should assess how it has added balance and synchronization to your life. Also, take the same principles of trial and error self-assessment and improve other dimensions of your life to increase positive mental stimulation to your mind, body, and spirit.

Points to Remember:

1. Policing will unintentionally force psychological, emotional, and physical changes which require an individual to find healthy balances to combat the unaware changes.

2. It is vital personally to assess or have a close friend, family member, and/or spouse to monitor your personality changes. Remember, moderation is the key.

3. It is essential to establish a life outside of policing to maintain a sense of normalcy.

Chapter 3 - Police Decision Making

Based on the overall number of calls for service police receive across the nation and compared to the negative incidents that are reported regarding police misconduct, it is accurate to imply that most police officers make good decisions on a regular basis. Of course, there is the small percentage of police who make poor decisions, and these behaviors affect the entire policing community. The negative incidents receive magnitudes of media attention because a police officer violated public trust and appeared to fail the community. Understandably, there must be accountability for the behaviors that police display and the implications of their actions.

Situational Circumstances

To approach this dilemma of police decision-making, there are several environmental factors that could affect police officer's behavior such situational circumstances, training, and conscious/unconscious decision-making. It is equally important to represent the unknown behaviors that occur between police and citizens during calls for service. Before processing the actual decision-making of a police officer, it is incumbent to assess the police officer's state of mind before arriving on a scene. This is a general analysis, but there is a need to explore several areas to gain an understanding.

One of the most challenging aspects of police work is the situational circumstances police officers encounter. Both academic literature and law enforcement communities debated the term routine, when referring to police patrol duties. After profound research, both parties agreed and refuted the term "routine calls for service." It is of equal importance to realize calls communicated over the radio may sound similar, but every call is different, presenting variables of uniqueness.

Frequently, police respond to calls for service that position them in a reactive mode and disadvantageous situations. Research has shown that suspects often have a predetermined state of mind before they interact with police. Police normally operate in a delayed 5 to 7-second reaction gap to a suspect's behavior. Within that 5 to 7 second timeframe, police must mentally process the suspect's actions and respond appropriately to the stimuli.

During a patrol shift, a police officer may experience these emotional surges several times with an 8-hour tour. In this situation, it is difficult to judge or attempt to internalize a police officer's actions in real time. Though unfair, I think people often forget that police are humans that have emotions such as fear, anxiety, anger, and make mistakes like the rest of society. There are some who will judge police actions with ease from the comfort of an office working on a written report, statements, and scenarios without real time presence of danger involved. This is the complexity of the job that police officers must learn how to master. Police are tasked to perform their jobs effectively in a natural setting that has a presence of danger while being mindful of the rights of the person creating the danger. Therefore, constant stress-induced training is imperative for the police department and police officer to respond satisfactorily when confronted with these types of situations.

Training

Conversely, when a police officer's actions require an explanation, those seeking to support or challenge police actions review police department training records. Training courses are the police department's mandated guidelines to establish how police officers operate and perform under state laws. Although training is designed to assure that police operate with the police department's guideline, there appears to be varying opinions on the transferability to practical field experience. Training for police officers should be relevant and up to date. Often, police departments are delayed in presenting police officers with trainings that prepare them for the constantly changing trends they encounter.

This next section is awkward to write, difficult to explain, but I realize it is a needed topic of conversation for the profession. It is a dilemma that most police departments would like to avoid or never have to respond to the unfavorable actions of a police officer's decision-making. Police can perform one hundred things correctly, but that one negative incident will overshadow all good deeds. As I always stated, I am not here to judge, pretend to have all the answers or say I had a perfect OPS record (Office Professional Standard). We are simply here to learn, exchanges ideas, and attempt to prevent future mistakes.

The ultimate question remains can training prevent police from making poor decisions? For those that have been in the policing profession for some time or even rookies, we have heard the stories of police officers committing unethical acts such as excessive use of force, unethical behaviors, drug offenses, and domestic violence issues. Whatever the offense, the line of ethics has been crossed, and police credibility is destroyed. While conducting this research, I studied the conscious/unconscious decision-making in regard to police related decision-making. This is a problematic subject to address due to several external situational factors, and each case encompasses different variables.

After interviewing various public safety scholars and gaining insight on their perspective of conscious decision-making. I realized a simple notion that all the police training presented during the police academy and yearly in-service training couldn't replace police officers utilizing common sense. Often, the legal troubles that a police officer encounters are from a lack of exercising fundamental thinking. Throughout my career, I always reflected on the phrase "common sense is not always common," but a level of thoughtfulness must be shown when serving and protecting the public. Simple rules

apply when encountering with the public, treat the public

how you want to be treated and represent your police

department. Many police officers would feel outraged if

their family members were subjected to the recent

behaviors of some police.

Currently, as of the mid-2014 thru 2017 period,

many police officers across the nation are failing in

decision-making. I have interviewed several police

chiefs and public safety officials. Their views vary on

the reasons for the behaviors that police officers display.

One chief stated, "maybe we are not focusing training on

the specific problems that the police officers encounter."

He seemed to think that the police training was behind

the learning curve and police departments are always

attempting to catch up on cultural understanding.

We have entered an anxious political

environment where citizens don't have confidence in the

police to perform their jobs fairly within all

communities. Most people have witnessed the significant differences in which various groups of people have been treated by the police. It doesn't take a genius to realize that a police department doesn't teach these behaviors. Of course, the police department will be under scrutiny from the community for allowing the police officer to remain on the department.

After there is a negative interaction involving the police, there is always the why series of questions. Why didn't the police do this, that, or another action? Questions arise, why does there appear to be a disparity in the way minority groups are treated? Here is my disclaimer, every case is different, which means that they should be judged on an individual basis and not grouped into one compartment. Often, during these interactions that generate a negative media outrage, both the police officer and citizen could have managed the situation differently. This discussion pertains to the police officers who seem to purposefully enforce excessive, commit wrongful acts to citizens, or mistreat certain diverse cultures. Professionally, I have brainstormed many theories, interviewed and conducted research on police behaviors. I solicited the input of Dr. Arcella Trimble of the Peak Development Group to theorize the various manners police interact with citizens.

In most cases, there is a stimulus to create a cause and effect reaction. In policing, the stimuli can be generated from a working environment, which police have repeated experiences in a natural setting. Hence, we revisited the foundation of functions of behaviors. There are four functions of behavior that explain why people behave in a certain manner. Most people will fall into one of these categories:

- Escape- An individual behaves to get out of something he/she does not want to do.

- Attention Seeking- An individual behaves to get attention from people around them.

- Seeking Access to Materials- An individual behaves to get something or preferred activity

- Sensory Stimulation- An individual behaves in a way because it feels good to them.

Upon revisiting the functions of behavior, we discovered there was another function that has been added. Social scientist added the "Power" function of behavior, and it is the most befitting function to police behavior.

- Power- An individual behaves to have power over a person or situation.

The word power associated with police officers can be taken in various manners but is normally perceived in a negative manner. Earlier in the book, we discussed the emotional tolls of policing which creates different changes within an individual police officer. Police will experience dissimilar emotions, and at times they will have issues processing emotions. Power is one of those emotions that can consciously or unconsciously change police.

The key is controlling the conscious and unconscious emotions associated with police power. Consciously, most police realize the power of their presence and how it alters public settings. Internally, this can be intoxicating and at times influence police attitudes. Unconsciously, police must remain thoughtful of the power they possess. Many police should dissuade several traits such as arrogance, vocal tone of conversations, and become aware approachable. These traits are purposeless to the profession and perpetrate pre-existing stereotypes. Before you throw burning stakes at police implying that this is an excuse for police to abuse their authority, let's take a few steps back, and review the characteristics of most police while creating a baseline to establish a level of understanding.

Most police officers possess an Alpha male personality with a high level of personal confidence which is needed to perform the job. Combine those personality traits with the power naturally associated with policing can generate a dangerous synergy. Fundamentally, I believe this is a root to many of the negative interactions between police and citizens. Police must mentally have the proper emotions in place when they exercise their power to balance controlling a situation versus abusing power. Currently, we live in a society where past police norms are challenged, and facts are checked by citizens for validity. These citizens challenge the police due to a lack of trust in past police interactions.

When most facts checkers interact with the police, they are not personally challenging police for a physical confrontation. They are challenging the system which is way beyond the police span of control, but police perceive it as a personal disregard for their authority. In most cases, they are not attempting to be a jerk, this is our new society, where everything is questioned. Policing hasn't transitioned with this paradigm shift in society. Thus, the wrong emotions are often in place creating a bad combination.

Consequently, police officers may respond back to these challenges with an elevated level of force, when a calmer emotional posture may resolve the situation. Most people are looking for someone with the power to listen, and police happen to be most accessible to most citizens. Police should allow people the opportunity to vent while possibly providing serviceable feedback. Many people ask questions because they truly want answers, somehow thinking the police are the ones who have a solution to all their problems. We both agreed that the training academy is where the foundation is created to change the police department and police officer's mentality. Others believe that a lack of cultural understanding is a barrier that obstructs communication which may funnel to aspects of poor decision-making.

Cultural Diversity

One approach to reduce poor decision-making with new police officers is to introduce cultural competency courses in the police academy. There need to be blocks of instruction that are only dedicated to understanding cultural competency within minority communities. It is not enough to know about a culture, but police need to go beyond that to develop a level of understanding of the people. Another approach will be understanding the conscious/unconscious thought process of police officers. In both circumstances, there may be an initial discord until a level of understanding can be developed.

Research has shown that many police departments unknowingly lack the knowledge and skills to adequately serve culturally diverse populations. I'm not implying that police departments don't have resources to address mainstream media issues or make valid efforts to address cultural issues. Nonetheless, most police departments haven't concisely addressed a cultural methodology to provide services to diverse populations. It is the responsibility of the police department to be knowledgeable of cultural diversities and issues that emerge from each group.

There are distinctive characteristics with each cultural group beyond the visible biological and social features. The police department must gain in-depth knowledge by learning and understanding cultural complexities. As it relates to police interactions, many cultures historically as well as currently have a mistrust of police. The mistrust of police should not offend police nor defend the problems of different cultures, however, be the catalyst for change to begin to erode layers of mistrust. Remember, it is easy to be the superior stakeholder with power in this interaction. Therefore, police must be conscious of their attitudes when interacting with the public. Police must dispose of the us against them attitude.

On the surface, most police officers assume they can work and effectively communicate with all ethnic cultures or individuals from varying minority demographics. The act of communicating may be possible under conditions when stress is not induced. The level of comfort changes when stress is induced, authority is challenged, and decisions must be made in actual time. Under these conditions, the true morality, beliefs, and values of a police officer reveal themselves.

Therefore, it is important to recognize the difference in people, cultures, and develop a relationship not an inferior interpretation of a culture. Once a simple fraction of understanding is generated, that may help establish a dialogue between police and the community. Let's be honest, I am aware that police will not reach all people, but the effort will show sincerity to the community. That alone will change some attitudes of some people you serve.

Regardless of varying opinions that have been formulated from the actions of the police, the responsibility falls directly on their shoulders, police are held to a higher standard. I have developed my own theory, intertwined with professional experiences. I studied various police cases that involved conscious decision-making and negative outcomes from police. Not to play Monday evening quarterback, but many officers could have made different decisions that would have produced a better result. Then, I reflected upon their training, which most police departments provide a proficient level of training. Like many organizations within our society, some police department will be more progressive with training than other police departments.

The origin of many problems often occurs during a situational circumstance when a possible challenge of police authority is perceived by a police officer. In many cases, police will display a show of force when they can calmly defuse a situation. Most people aren't personally looking to always challenge police, but in search for solutions during emotional crisis. The unspoken communication that is lost between police and citizens creates friction. This is a discomfited situation because police are trained to confront and adapt the challenges of the community.

Most cases involve male police officers and most male police officers will meet force with force. Police seek to command control over situations and physically impose their authority. The suspect in many cases has exercised poor judgment and is attempting to escape the consequences of their immediate actions. I will not explore the varying actions that could happen between police and citizens because every scenario is different. I would like to focus on a more proactive thought process. It is important for police to keep their emotions and responses within the scope of their training. Again, I will utilize my disclaimer, but I am not making excuses for police or lessening citizen actions. As police, you are expected to be in control over all situations, no matter the circumstance.

Conscious and Unconscious Decision Making

There are constant debates on whether police behaviors are conscious or unconsciously driven. Notably, this topic is difficult to conclude, due to the variations of social scientist theories. Some think simply discussing issues may alter the police thought process of the poor conscious or unconscious decision-making. I disagree with this theory since many of our conscious thoughts are developed through life experiences.

Professionally, I feel some police have distorted perceptions of minority cultures, allowing for myths to distort interactions and the lack of cultural awareness to understand. Truth be told, these actions are normal to a degree. Both police officers and regular citizens have some issues functioning outside of their natural social network. After many years, we as a nation still have a fear of openly discussing racial issues. There seems to be an ugliness surrounded around the word race, and a fear of offending other cultures. The true offense is honestly ignoring the issues of other by marginalizing their differences. Many of our unintentional moral thoughts, values, and distinctiveness derive from being diverse.

Consequently, our uncharted path of childhood to adulthood affects our conscious opinions of other ethnic groups. A substantial body of research has shown that working in a normal casual multicultural environment can create stress for the various cultural groups involved. Focus that similar concept to policing in a multicultural environment that further exposes a person's anxiety, fears, and lack of understanding for both police and community. There are several psychological external barriers that must be developed to assist with dealing with being a service provider in a multicultural environment. Therefore, we must try to simplify and illuminate issues of potential risk.

A cultural assessment of a social environment can be difficult to effectively analyze without being a vested stakeholder. In this circumstance, a vested stakeholder would be affected somehow by the changes in the community. It is important to realize that often some community residential stakeholders have minimal control, resources, or significant tools to change their immediate condition. Often, vested stakeholders are constantly reoriented with their reality while understanding the perception of their reality is viewed poorly by outsiders. Moreover, consciously or unconsciously, people tend to make negative assumptions of a culture based upon their current social living condition.

An issue is the proper balance between cultural understanding and maintaining conscious or unconscious thoughts by police. It is easy to deviate from this balance without the critical thinking skills developed from a heightened sense of awareness. Arguably, a police department is a total contradiction to its own structure, since communication within the organization isn't a strong point. Research has shown that some police have difficulties communicating in urban patrol environments.

Conversely, repeated experiences in this environment will generate various stressors. Unfortunately, police officers may unconsciously develop negative thoughts, stereotypes, and opinions towards citizens residing in the community.

Police officers unknowingly form a social cognition approach which relates to the way they socially view the community, create community norms, and establish their policing style. Basically, some may think it is acceptable to patrol the environment parallel to how the community interacts with each other. This would not be a suggested mode of approach when policing in a diverse community. This type of police action would further isolate the community while tarnishing an already damaged relationship. Moreover, police should focus on those controversial moments during police and citizen's interactions.

Earlier, we acknowledged that policing can be a fast pace environment that encompasses continuous emotional surges. Ham and Bos (2010) offered an individual's judgments are primarily developed through fast and unconscious social-cognitive processes. This concept illustrates another interconnection that police endure when making decisions during interactions. Therefore, a potential strategy for overcoming this action should help police before interacting with citizens. This is a rather simple idea that may ultimately reduce some poor interactions. After a police officer receives a call for service, then they begin to mentally process the call for service. Before they arrive on the scene, police need to formulate an intermediate decision plan. Police need to mentally recalibrate their social cognitive process.

Previously, we discussed that social cognition is developed from repeatedly functioning in a certain environment. The concept of an intermediate decision plan would require the police officer to rethink their normal approach responding to a call. This is not a statement to jeopardize your safety, but begin to think about options other than physical force to reduce negative interactions. In short, when you have spare time, you should mentally practice scenarios in your mind to properly diffuse situations. Police must develop a next level thinking process, even if they don't want to do it. This simple thought process will benefit police officers in the overall process of community relations.

If possible, show the citizens of your community that you are a regular person. I have professionally used this approach as a police officer, and it totally changes the attitude of the citizens who I encountered. Your attitude towards citizens that you encounter will be spoken among the community. Believe me; the community has a social network that discusses police officers who patrol the community and how they treat citizens. Word of mouth in the community can be your best tool to build trust in the community. Enough odds are already stacked within the profession, so you need to build as many positive relationships as obtainable.

Points to Remember

1. All police decisions will not be favorable to
    the public, but they should be lawfully fair
    to the public.

2. Policing is a constantly evolving occupation;
    therefore, police officers must understand
    their craft and the people they serve.
    Become culturally aware of the communities
    you serve.

3. Police officers should regularly conduct a
    self-analysis to make sure they have the
    proper emotions in place to fairly serve the
    community.

Chapter 4 - Saving Yourself

Many police officers enter the profession with a notion to help others or improve their community. The profession has a profound trait of revolving fate and necessitating many police require help. Hopefully, you have enough awareness to recognize that you may need assistance to function with adequate normalcy. My disclaimer, "I am not saying overall all police have issues, but the job does alter your personality." Most importantly, these changes can have a direct impact on your family such as your spouse, children, and yourself.

The changes within a police officer's personality develop over a time, but their behavior change can be seen slowly in various segments of their life. With respect to all police officers, it is almost inevitable that you will change to parallel your work environment. For example, police officers that work in a fast-paced environment that requires quick decision-making and constant adrenaline surges. These actions become part of the daily work routine. When repeated enough, this unknowing become part of your blueprint for decision making in your personal life. Police begin to make decisions with their personal lives as if they are at work, which is not conducive to a healthy balance. Decisions made on the job may lack certain empathy, emotional passion, and unyielding compromise due to the disposition police must maintain. This approach will not lead to a successful personal life with your family members. To avoid making these pitfall decisions that may generate a downward spiral in your personal life, there are some preventive precautious steps that are important for police to reflect upon.

This is a common saying but always put your family interest first. Often, police get so consumed with the job that they sometimes lose focus. In some cases, the job has a higher priority than their family life. You should police to provide a living but live for your family. I recall being in a roll call before starting my patrol shift. My sergeant always told stories on a regular basis. This day, the story referenced, remember you guys are a position number to the city so protect yourself because you are the most important person to your family. When you think about it, agency's personnel department fills position number when the position necessitates.

To the agency, police are simply position number that requires fulfilling to meet the needs of the budget. I am not saying the city government does not value its employees but remember you should place family first. The government will always place business first and expendable commodities in a prioritized order. Police officers need to adopt a business approach to their police work. They should think of themselves as their own CEO, and no one has a better interest in their stakeholdings than themselves.

CEO of You

The CEO mindset is vital when making decisions during your patrol duties, especially when interacting with the public. If police officers make unfavorable decisions that garner negative public

attention or cost the city government revenue, the police

department may isolate themselves or refute the

decision-making of the police officer. Thus, absolving

some level of personal responsibility for the police

officers' actions and placing more of the onus on the

individual's actions. In other words, the government will

do what is best for them so you may need to follow their

pattern. The self-preservation of your namesake, your

family, financial security, and career promotion should

always be at the forefront of your mind. The CEO

mindset should be your constant mode of operation.

The changing of a police officer's mindset is

often difficult for a police officer to master. Not saying

this in a negative behavior, because police are designed

to be in control of situations. Initially, it may be difficult

releasing the control of power which has been ingrained

since their date of hire. Yet, it is beneficial for the police

officer's overall mental, physical, and psychological

balance to expand their horizon which can be achieved

by releasing some control. This is where you conduct a mirror test and assess the areas of your life that need improvement. Personal growth beyond the scope of policing will reduce some of the stressors associated with policing.

The overall goal of a police officer should be to achieve Allostasis in their lives. McEwen and Wingfield (2003) described Allostasis as the process of achieving stability by means of healthy psychological and/or behavioral transformation. Moderate levels of stress are required to generate stimulated learning, mental muscles, and potentially excelling in certain situations. A healthy balance should be the quest of life that all people should strive for.

To achieve this healthy balance in life, you should explore different options and make constant changes in your life. We are all different, so the paths taken are limitless such as continuing education, hobbies, fitness, or venturing to start a new business.

Whatever the venture these activities require mental stimulation not related to an environmental hazardous based stimulus. Of course, there is stress in all areas of life, but it is vital that the stressor is not public safety related. I personally think that there are two areas of interest that police should explore financial management and continuing education.

Another aspect of developing the CEO mindset is financial preparation. I will be the first to mention that police across America are underpaid. The salary that police receive is not equivalent to their contribution they make daily within various communities. The average police salary is normally below the cost of living in most cities, and many police can't afford to reside in the city they patrol.

It is vital for police officers to wisely manage their finances from the beginning of the career. Often in this book, I like to use my personal disclaimer. Trust, there were periods in my policing career where I made brainless decisions with my money such as partying, heavy dating rotation, traveling, and spur of the moment roads trips with the fellas. Wait, these road trips did build positive lifelong friendships.

Being that a police officer salary starts in the low 40's, it is important to financially plan for the future. This is in general, but the average police retirement is sixty percent of their top 3 years of salary. The overall cost of living continues to rise in the cities that police officers serve while many police salaries remain stagnant. Therefore, police need to invest wisely to obtain a comfortable lifestyle during retirement. It is extremely disheartening to see a police officer that retires after thirty years of service and is still working extra jobs to meet their financial obligations.

As police officers, you must stop making Chapter 13 life decisions and think you can recover from it later. Police are not doctors, attorneys, IT personnel, or financial advisers where your salary will increase with productivity or substantial yearly bonuses. Police must stop purchasing houses, cars, and/or whatever personal vice that extends beyond past their financial resources. Then work extra jobs to no end, attempting to pay for our personal vices.

Now, this is where the plot gets thicker, and a mirror test needs to be conducted. I will use my personal disclaimer: I should have conducted the test on myself many times during my policing career. As your own CEO, you are the best asset to yourself, but often, we don't treat ourselves in that manner. Again, the profession generates this superhero mentality within your DNA. Thus, we carry this invincible ego, but our poor personal decision-making becomes our kryptonite. This section is mainly for male police officers since statistics state that female police officers usually make better decisions.

The myth that women like a man in uniform appears to be a true proclamation. The police uniform often gives the average police officer attention that he may not normally receive. At times, this sudden attention or ability to don a uniform fogs male police officer's thoughts. Basically, we buy into our own hype of being greater than what we really are. As police officers, I would like to think of us as special, not different from others.

Often, we make choices without utilizing good judgment. In many cases, we involve ourselves with women from bars, clubs, and calls for services to become your girlfriend or spouse. Many of these women are looking for someone to save them from themselves. Unfortunately, with the mindset that has been indoctrinated since the date of hire, we swoop in and think that we can save the beautiful women (I meant the world). Words to live by: A police badge can get you a lot of women, but women have also taken a lot of badges.

We are developing the CEO mindset; thus, it is vital to realize when choosing a spouse or partner that it takes a special type of woman to marry or seriously date a police officer. Many women are infatuated with the idea of a police officer as a partner, but may not truly understand all the aspects of a police officer personality. Therefore, as a police officer, we have failed marriages, toxic relationships, and multiple children. These decisions cost police financially, and kids require eighteen to twenty-one years of financial obligation. Remember the starting salary is in the low 40's, and it can only be divided in so many ways.

Therefore, police need to realize the importance of aligning with women who will add to their goals, future endeavors, and (personal)organization. You need to seek a woman or partner who has logical goals and is actively taking steps to achieve those goals. For example, you do not want a woman saying her goal is to be the CEO of IBM, but she never completed college and hates interacting with people. You are a CEO of your own company; lip service doesn't pay the bills, and a woman that is a financial burden is a threat to your organization. Add someone to your organization who inserts value to your stock and has just as much to lose as yourself.

Police are like many other Americans: we all want what we can't have and buy things we can't afford. Financially extending yourself beyond your salary is detrimental to you personally and professionally. The burden of financial stress can affect your job performance and decision-making at work. It may seem insignificant to owe creditors or have your paycheck spent without money left over after paying your bills. But this does have a conscious influence on your mood and may influence your judgment. Reflect for a few seconds. You overall feel better when you have money in your bank account, and your personal affairs are in order.

The Stages of Policing

Just as your policing career begins, it will also come to an end. The years of your career will escape faster than you realize, similar to many aspects of our lives. During your policing career, there will be challenges, high and lows, deaths of fellow police officers, and lifelong friendships developed. It is essential to conduct periodic assessments to successfully navigate a policing career. The average police career will be in four major stages (1) Development stage 1-5 years, (2) Active stage 5-10 years, (3) Transitional Stage 10-15 years, and (4) Exodus Stage 20 plus years.

Development Stage

It is difficult to understand the Art of Policing until fully working and responding to 911 calls for service. This is where you really get an opportunity to internally assess your skills and learn your own strengths as well as weakness. The strength and weakness of an individual will determine how they develop their personal policing style. The development stage, in my opinion, is the most important phase of your policing career. This stage will set the foundation on how you will be perceived by coworkers and most importantly the public you serve.

The understanding of policing will begin to develop as a police officer acclimates themselves to the community they serve. In many cases, police officers will not normally come from a background similar to the population they serve. Therefore, a learning curve will be generated, and a negotiated order of communication will need to be established. There will be a negotiated line of communication since the community may not be accustomed to your style of policing, manner of communication, and maybe contrast in demographic backgrounds. This can initially be mentally challenging, however, over time both stakeholders should learn to adapt to one another.

Psychologically, the most difficult transition can be adapting to new coworkers and the culture of policing. Even though we are adults, similar to children, we still desire to be liked amongst our peers and being able to handle the pressures of the job is a part of the subculture. So as rookies, I think most of us presented the persona that we could manage the job but had high levels of anxiety until a comfort level was established. This is one of the initial forms of work-related stress police officers experience. The learning curve of attempting to learn from veteran police officers, combined with mentally attempting to maintain your anxieties from the job.

Despite the burden of being a new police officer, this is a time they should really cherish. The early stages of policing can be humbling, yet you receive a wealth of knowledge from the veterans. Positive and negative veterans will share experiences that can assist in navigating the police department, extending your career, surviving the job, and getting promoted. This information will guide new police officers to the next stage of their career if they chose to continue the journey.

Active Stage

The active stage is one of the most important and intriguing towards a police officer's career. In the active phase of policing, the officer has gained a vast amount of knowledge and understands their role. The officer is immersed in the culture, understanding the needs of the community, goals of the patrol district, and has developed their own style of policing. Some officers may progress faster than others because this is the run and gun phase which attracts people to a policing career. At this juncture in a police officer's career, they are consciously aware of the politics entrenched within the police department. Politics is a key part of policing that is rarely discussed in the police academy, but it can ascend or descend a policing career.

Essentially, police officers at this phase have several options they need to explore to determine their future. Some police officers will realize after a few years the policing careers isn't exactly what they anticipated and explore other professions. Others chose to remain with the police department, exploring options to advance into different divisions or continuing to remain in the police district responding to 911 calls for service. Another group of police officers will attempt to become detectives and work in specialized units.

The uniqueness of responding to 911 calls is the exposure to the variety of crimes such as robbery, domestic violence, burglary, auto theft, and assaults. Inexperienced, police officers gain firsthand knowledge of each crime, which present various aspects of each crime. Notable lessons are learned from these experiences, which will guide you through the remainder of your career. Opportunities exist to build on this foundation and make these lesson tools that can transfer to management skills.

Like most journeys that require a substantial amount of dedicated time, effort, and sacrifice there will be downfalls during the journey with several periods of high and low moments. Research has shown that between 5 to 7 years of service, some police officers may commit a major unethical act or behavior. The key to this pattern is determining if police officers are consciously or unconsciously making decisions that are violations of the law. Some unethical decisions have ramifications that could result in disciplinary actions such as suspensions, terminations, legal compensation, and personal compensation to the party involved.

A Social Scientist debated for years with several theories generating the behaviors that some police officer exhibit. One of the theories is police officers within the 5 to 7 years of service are familiar with the police department and recognize to navigate the department's rules. It may be unspoken among police culture, but police sometimes like to test their power against the organization. Thus, this intoxicating power can mystify a police officer's judgment and decision-

making. Ok, don't gasp at the next sentence but police

really like to test their limits. Once the parameters are

established, the do's & don'ts of the department; there

will be the police that likes to walk that thin line.

Another theory is the development of skilled

manipulation learned from working the streets. Young

police officers learn numerous lessons from policing the

streets, which will later influence their style of policing.

During these teachable movements, young police

officers are sometimes being outwitted, hustled,

challenged, lied too, and basically taught the culture of

the district they police. Lessons that the police academy

can't teach, but the knowledge gained only from walking

through the fire. Over time, the young police officers

will learn the tricks the streets taught, integrating

themselves in the streets. Redundancies occur in many

areas of policing which may create attitudes such as lack

of interest, over-eagerness to patrol, or unexpected

testing of morals.

To make this concept real, most people analyze the ending behaviors of a police officer who commits an unethical act. It is important to view all parts aspects of the behavior, prior to the ending result. As such, there must be a focus on the subtle changes that occurred initially. Some police officers may do minor things that will not align with a normal pattern of behavior. Often, co-workers may witness the behavior but may dismiss it as "he/she is a little off today or say he/she needs a few days off." This is the process of separating from ethical decision-making. Moreover, they may become comfortable in this pattern of behavior, enabling them to take more unethical risk.

To conclude, during this period, police officers must conduct constant self-awareness evaluations and take ownership of their actions. This is an undervalued practice that may have significant implications. During challenging times, police officers should take the initiative to deter negative consciously based decisions. Police train on tactics to get out of hazardous environments, yet fail to take this same approach to professional decision-making. Therefore, a strategic-based reflection should be performed projecting the possible result of negative actions. Police must think beyond themselves, realizing that their negative actions have consequences for others associated with them.

Of course, this does not apply to most police officers' career, but many police officers have made poor decisions, warranting this to be a worthy topic of research and debate. It is important to visualize a successful career and formulate strategic decisions to navigate your pathway to infinite possibilities. My disclaimer, not that I was perfect during my entire career, but your reputation is your best asset.

Transitional Stage

At this point in a career, a police officer has clearly chosen policing as a career. Most police officers have accomplished certain goals professionally and personally. The unique characteristic of policing at this stage should be the ability to translate field experience to departmental leadership. The outlook of the police department is primarily structured at this level. Another attribute developed at this level is the understanding of politics intertwined in policing. To reach upper management in a police department, an individual has generated a proven record of politics, field experience, and maintained harmonious relationships within the community with other public leaders.

Notably, I acknowledge that this level may be the most difficult phase of a police officer's career due to the politics. Prior to reaching this level of policing, past accomplishments were based upon job-related performances. This stage of a police career's success is built upon the influence of political relationships developed. The art of policing can be very challenging and constantly evolving. The political power of a police department can shift without warning, and be beyond the control of involved immediate stakeholders. In such a circumstance, a key technique to possess is the ability to be flexible, adaptable, and never compromise your integrity.

During my interview with a police chief, I asked how did you navigate the politics of policing. He replied, "I always stick to my principles and simply perform my job. If someone recognizes my work great and if not, I continue to perform my job." I personally have never been a chief of police, but I completely understand his approach. Simply perform your job, and what is meant for you, you will receive.

Typically, most political appointments in local government are selected in an attempt to appease community stakeholders. Therefore, it is important to recognize the benefits of forming a community partnership with all stakeholders in your community of service. Community partners can express their like or dislike for police officers beyond a specific patrol district to personnel members in upper management. It is often surprising the amount of power the "Ladies

Auxiliary of Flowers Association" possess and the ears their complaints reach. Again, policing is a non-mutual responsive atmosphere and love is very much conditional at this level. If interdependence is established, there are opportunities to advance within the police department.

Exodus

This phase of a policing career speaks volumes. Any police officer that reaches this milestone should be proud of themselves, thankful to their families, and memories that will last a lifetime. Police officers at this stage should always be smiling and counting down the days to retirement. Many are preparing for the next phase in their life. The journeys will vary depending upon the police officer's goal such as retiring completely, pursuing other opportunities in law enforcement, or some pursuing different professions.

As I am writing this, I reflected upon my former Field Training Officer (FTO) and his retirement. Before his Exodus stage, he went to a technical college and became a certified auto mechanic. Shortly after retiring, he opened his own shop and is happy fixing cars. It is important at this phase to have a transitional plan for retiring. A cardinal sin for many police officers preparing to retire is not solidifying a concrete play for life after policing. Whatever options you choose, properly prepare to prevent from experiencing stagnant periods of inactivity.

Points to Remember:

1. Always put your family before the job. The police department will survive without you.

2. Develop a CEO mindset; you are your own investment.

3. Don't make Chapter 13 decisions with your life; it takes too much time and energy to recover.

Afterthoughts

As I close out this book, I had various thoughts wondering if I covered all topics intended for my audience. My thoughts reflected upon a conversation that I had on a radio talk show regarding police reformation. The host asked before closing what advice I would give to the listeners and why it is important. I am an advocate for changing a police culture, so often I intertwine messages that can serve police officers, other professionals, and common everyday people. Overall, we innately mishandle many aspects of our lives, often creating unnecessary worries, anxieties, and/or complications by over analyzing life decisions. Hence, it is imperative to create a safe zone in your life to assess situations that will assist in managing your reality.

Managing your Reality

One of the best lessons I have learned in life is there will be many failures, and our victories will not always define you. I think as children most of our parents attempted to shelter us from the realities of life. Along the way, we skipped through life until we had that one obstacle which gut punched us with reality. For example, my first gut punch of reality was my first job, and my paycheck not covering my expenses. The entire time, I assumed a college degree would eradicate me from being broke living from paycheck to paycheck. I took for granted the sacrifices of my parents and realized the journey of life comes without instructions.

This premise will apply to most people at some point in their life. Like the old cliché, it doesn't matter how many times you get knocked down, but the key is to get back up. What I found is often people get stuck on one obstacle that gut punched them, and they never recovered from the blow. People tend to allow this one reality define them. It is important not to become disjointed by this stifling. Don't illuminate this problem to be more than what is presents in your life. Reclaim you pose and learn how to manage your reality. This philosophy is interrelated to many people's professional, personal life, and especially in policing.

From the onset of early police training, they ingrain young police officers with the strengths of the job. Rarely taught are the limitations or strategic diplomacy of policing. It is essential to recognize your limitations and develop a strategic deterrence to protect your vulnerabilities. This tool isn't utilized against citizens to create a divide between police and the community. It is to identify an alternative approach to habitual issues that are not currently addressed by the police department.

Your Reality

The objective of managing your reality is to minimize your negative interactions, develop a personally designed plan, and avoid further escalations of issues. At some point in your policing career or just in life, there will be a deficiency in self-fulfillment. This feeling is normal and happens to most people. There may be several reasons for these feelings, such as professional unhappiness, failure to meet life goals, financial uncertainty, and adult peer pressure. During these periods of shortcomings, it is vital to analyze your behaviors. I would like to reiterate this is a normal feeling for many people.

Would life not be amazing if it allowed us to foresee, prioritize, and minimize our negative interactions. Only if life provided us with the ability to proportionate a response with a delayed time which would allow us to gather our thoughts, instead of immediately responding with charged emotions. Think about all the decisions we would have made differently and mistakes that could have been avoided that has made an impact on your present status. While life doesn't always offer a clear framework to manage your reality, it does enable us with flexible options. Many of us have made poor choices, yet we can still find another path to get us back on course. Before we proceed like many products warnings on the market, results may vary, some options may not be desirable, but they will provide

workable options. This will also allow you time to

negotiate a more permanent long-term solution.

Since conception, man has always been involved

in some form of a disagreeing interaction. Traditionally,

these are low-intensity disagreements between two

stakeholders where a discontent of communication

evolves into an adversary relationship. Many years later,

we are still experiencing similar strife just as our

forefathers did before us. The problematic issue with

most relationships is securing a solid foundation to

function. This is where the simple becomes tricky

because we manage to make this hard. We continue to

see the same pattern of results because we repeat the

same cycle of behaviors.

Therefore, we must manage our boundaries over

specific acute core issues. Often, many conflicts are over

massive stockpiles of control issues, poor

communication, and misplaced egos. These variables

prohibit effective interactions which are illegitimate components to stabilize a secure foundation. Typically, in our daily lives, people disagree to win the control battles, but surprisingly the final prize isn't worth the war. We become so focused on proving a point that we lose concentration on the acute issue.

The acute issues aren't discovered until you acknowledge your true discontent and create a change course of action. With this new mindset, you can limit negative courses of action while negotiating your next progressive move; before you can effectively make any positive changes in life. I think a person should learn the Art of Listening rather than the practice of talking to simply reply. Generally, we are quick to assume we know how a person will respond, what they say, and often misperceiving the information. Many people find comfort in blaming others rather than taking charge of themselves.

What to do when you don't know what to do?

For most of us, the mirror test is a pain point. Being honest with ourselves and taking responsibility for their current role within their own situation can be difficult. Although, this is the first step in the right direction. Claiming ownership for your failures is often harder than the initial obstacle. Don't spend a lot of time galvanizing over your problem. Remember, every problem has a solution. You just have to find the correct approach to your issue. For example, if you have an issue with credit card debit which exceeds your monthly income to balance your financial needs. This problem may require canceling your credit card, reducing household spending, and seeking additional employment to supplement your income. This situation may not be ideal for the person that has to burden the responsibility, but it is a step in the positive direction towards a goal.

Create a plan that works for you. Don't judge your progress against the next person. Your plan can only be determined by you since you will be the person burdening the load. I would seek positive mentors and seek knowledge that would add to your journey. Again, remain realistic with your goals while monitoring your limitations. This allows you to remain on pace, leaving room for setbacks, but the resiliency to keep moving forward. Also, it allows you function in the mindset of understanding your life is broader than your current state of environment. A special emphasis should always be placed entirely on tangible actions to overcome all obstacles in life.

Defending your Boundaries

There is an old saying "people and places can get you into a lot of bad situations." Often, we allow others too much negative appreciation in our personal space and allow them to continue to expand their territory without permission. For this reading, negative appreciation is allowing an unhealthy source such as people or lifestyles to function in your daily life. They consume large space, yet, their value depreciates your internal framework. Why do they exist in our space, better yet how did they get here? Well, you can probably reexamine the gut punch that knocked you to the canvas. When you were on the canvas, you may have found someone else on the floor too. Emotionally, you thought maybe someone feels my pain and understands your current situation. At this point, you were emotionally and mentally unbalanced, thus, making poor decisions.

We all at some point have lost focus with poor decision-making, which makes it difficult to get on the path. Subsequently, you begin to search for an excuse on why you lost focus instead of the reason you lost focus. During these desperate periods, we often look to others to provide us with direction on your path when ultimately, they don't know the course of your past journey. This action is called unity in the wrong direction, the gathering of two or more people without a solid foundation making poor decisions. People together often don't match, but sometimes in a certain space within life, they perfectly fit causing each other self-inflicted pain.

Dr. Measha Dancy offers the following explanation for various interactions: Energy is everywhere and makes up everyone and everything. Every human being is composed of all forms of energy from the most physical and dense, like our bodies, to the extrasensory and least dense, like our thoughts and emotions. Ideally, this physical, mental and emotional energetics are connected and free flowing within and around us. In regards to relationships and why a person may draw a certain type of person or situation to themselves can be explained by the various energetics we hold. Have you ever noticed that you or a person you know continually finds themselves in the same irritating type of situation repeatedly? Or that they get into similar unsuccessful relationships or have interactions with the same toxic people? These interactions usually cause the person some level of pain or disappointment. The reason this is so prevalent is because there are many people who harbor low vibrational energetics within their subconscious. The subconscious is the part of the psyche that is hidden from our conscious awareness. These low vibrational energies were usually created through some type of physical, mental, and/or emotional childhood trauma. When this type of trauma occurs, a "crack" is created in our previously free flowing energy field. This energetic crack is like a stagnation of energy, or blockage of energetic flow remains at a low level, or very dense, vibrational state. While the rest of us grow physically, mentally, and emotionally in other ways, that particular energy remains stagnant. And because it is not within our conscious purview, our unawareness allows for it to send out an energetic frequency that calls in people and situations of a similar low vibration. The ultimate purpose of this is so that energy can call attention to itself, come into our conscious awareness and allow for healing to occur. Relationships and situations of this type can lead to exponential self-awareness and spiritual growth.

Overcoming your Obstacle

After stability is established, a primary mission for yourself should be ensuring a reserve plan, forming a partnership, and moving with a strategic purpose. Although you may have overcome your obstacle, there should be ongoing steps to prevent a relapse in poor decision-making. There should be an outline set for your future goals with critical elements established and the time to act is now. Hence, you must realize only you can create a better future for yourself.

One of the most insightful goals should be forming a positive partnership. Understanding the concept that positive progression and an excellent foundation is shaped by critical partnership infrastructure. This is a broad approach, but you should embrace relationships that improve your opportunities. Partner with people that are achieving in innovative ways beyond your current capabilities. Do not allow this process to intimidate, but tailor your skills to embark upon your fullest potential. To make this concept real, you should support your efforts with a trial and error period within other social networks. At the end of the day, it is about you achieving by interchanging platforms while finding a suitable support system.

Making your moves count

Opportunities to capitalize on positive foundations are rare instead of the norm in life. During this period, you must be prepared for this moment. Too often, people waste time, energy, and mental capacity in situations that don't improve your overall personal infrastructure. In many cases, people will spend unnecessary years in partnerships that will never produce value on another level. Years later, you reflect on how time you lost with this stagnant circumstance.

We should maximize our investments within ourselves. We must be smarter about developing strategic moves that count towards your personal investment, while still thinking forward in an imaginative manner to continue self-improvement. We should always tighten our partnerships while constantly assessing your infrastructure. It is important to expand relationships when appropriate still improving areas of weakness. Only you can analyze the area that needs the most improvement in your life.

As I conclude this book, I would like to exercise my disclaimer and advice that I don't have all the answers. This book was designed to address issues that I have witnessed, researched or educational theories that could provide awareness. I believe it is an honor and a life changing experience to be a police officer. Of course, like many things in life, we take good police officers for granted and focus attention on the bad police officers. Police will probably never get the credit, recognition, or compensation they rightfully deserve. An instructor in my police academy class told us one day, if you are looking to get rich, you chose the wrong profession. But if you want a job where you give a lot, get minimal return, and a profession with very conditional love. Welcome to Policing.

Contributors

Arcella J. Trimble, Ph.D.- is a Licensed Psychologist, Coach, and Master Teacher. She is an expert in Learning, Behavior Modifications, Research, and Training. With 20 + years of experience. Dr. Trimble has worked with clients in mental health facilities, businesses, schools, and private practice. Through the use of data collection, assessment, and uniquely crafted experimental learning and behavior activities, Dr. Trimble successfully enhances outcomes for individuals, groups, and businesses.

Measha Dancy, M.D.- is a physician, yoga instructor, and a certified Holistic Health Coach. After practicing traditional medicine in Atlanta for over 12 years, she made the decision to follow her calling to learn alternative and ancient methods of healing. She is currently working to develop her future holistic wellness center.

References

Ham, J., & Van den Bos, K. (2010). On Unconscious
Morality: The effects of unconscious thinking on
moral decision making. *Social Cognition,* 28(1),
74-83.

McEwen, B.S., & Wingfield, J.C. (2003). The Concept
of Allostasis in Biology and Biomedicine.
Hormones and Behavior, 43(1), 2-15.